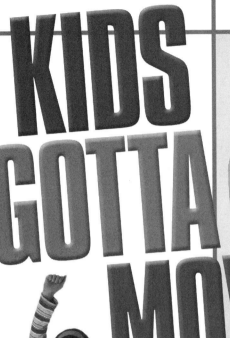

KIDS GOTTA MOVE!

by john jacobson

a dictionary of dance for young performers

ISBN 0-634-08237-X

HAL•LEONARD® CORPORATION
7777 W. BLUEMOUND RD. P.O. BOX 13819 MILWAUKEE, WI 53213

Copyright © 2004 by HAL LEONARD CORPORATION
International Copyright Secured   All Rights Reserved

No Part of this publication may be reproduced in any form or by any means without the prior written permission of the Publisher.

Visit Hal Leonard Online at
www.halleonard.com

INTRODUCTION

I have completely lost count as to how many letters, phone calls and e-mails I receive each year asking me to demonstrate "on the phone" a particular gesture or dance move that was suggested in one of our choral publications. By now, everybody seems to have figured out that L means "left", R means "right" and any song can be successfully staged if you have a bag of tricks that includes the Hand Jive and a Clap Burst! But, hardly anybody truly knows how to properly execute The Cabbage Patch, The Smurf or the California Raisins! Imagine that!

In 1997, with the help of my friends at Hal Leonard Corporation, I published a book and video collection called *Dictionary of Dance.* We called it The Ultimate Guide For The Choral Director. We hope that it has helped upper level junior high, high school and college song and dance programs enhance their performances with some of the moves explained and demonstrated within. We felt it was particularly helpful for classic Show Choirs comfortable with moderate to highly sophisticated dance routines and musical productions. It contained nearly 500 terms from the "Basic Soft Shoe" to "Shuffle off to Buffalo." It did NOT however, include the Cabbage Patch!

Kids Gotta Move! is designed for teachers of younger singers from Kindergarten through Junior High School. In this collection, we have included 100 of my favorite moves that I know from years of experience work wonderfully for young singers. Best of all, with the advent of technology we are able to include in this collection a DVD that allows me to demonstrate these moves to you and your students LIVE, (well almost.) It certainly will be easier to explain and learn than over the phone! With the use of this glossary, you will be able to refer to this book and DVD whenever you see a staging suggestion in one of our publications that you do not understand.

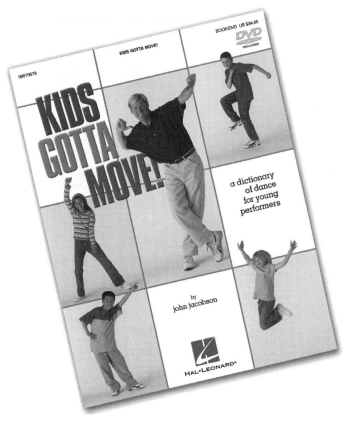

Acknowledgements:
Student Dancers: Jordan Yentz and Adam Steffan from Wauwatosa, Wisconsin

ASSESSMENT

Another great use for this publication is that you can challenge your students to learn all of the 100 terms and related moves and easily track their progress as they do so. Simply name a move and have them execute it for you. This kind of assessment is fun and breeds success both in the classroom and on the stage. At the back of the book I've included a list of most of the terms and even a few simple combinations of steps that you can use like a Charades Game. Copy them. Cut them into slips of paper. Put them in a hat and let a student pull one out. Whatever they see on the slip of paper they have to perform in front of the class as the class guesses the move. You can decide if this is a reward or a punishment, but it should make for a lot of fun learning in the music room!

In our constant quest to get kids wiggling in the right direction, I hope that you find **Kids Gotta Move!** a helpful and rewarding addition to your teaching materials.

– *John Jacobson*

ABOUT THE AUTHOR

John Jacobson
Music Educator, Choreographer, Entertainment Consultant
Member ASCAP, MENC, ACDA

In October of 2001 President George Bush named John Jacobson a Point of Light award winner for his "dedication to providing young people involved in the arts opportunities to combine music, charitable giving and community service." John is the founder and volunteer president of America Sings! Inc., a non-profit organization that encourages young performers to use their time and talents for community service.

With a bachelor's degree in Music Education from the University of Wisconsin-Madison and a Master's Degree in Liberal Studies from Georgetown University, John is recognized internationally as a creative and motivating speaker for teachers and students involved in choral music education. He is the author and composer of many musicals and choral works that have been performed by millions of children worldwide, as well as educational videos and tapes that have helped music educators excel in their individual teaching arenas, all published exclusively by Hal Leonard Corporation.

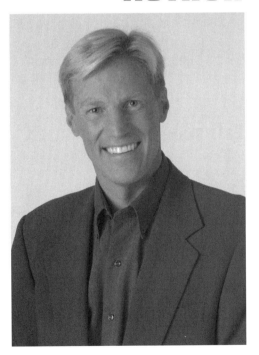

John has staged hundreds of huge music festival ensembles in his association with Walt Disney Productions and directed productions featuring thousands of young singers including NBC's national broadcast of the Macy's Thanksgiving Day Parade, presidential inaugurations and more. John stars in children's musical and exercise videotapes, most recently the series Jjump! A Fitness Program for Children and is the Senior Contributing Writer for John Jacobson's Music Express, an educational magazine for young children published by Hal Leonard Corporation.

GLOSSARY

Axle – Pretend to be skating first left (L), then right (R), then twice to the left (L). Repeat pattern to the other side, skating R L R R. The hands are usually complementing the move, stretching as if you are pulling a thread.

AXLE

Back Step (BS) – First, step back on one foot and then forward on the other, with a weight change as you move from one foot to the other.

Ball Change (BC) / Kick Ball Change (KBC) – Step on the ball of one foot and then shift your weight to the other foot. While similar to a back step, this movement is usually associated with an uneven rhythm where the step on the ball of the one foot is shorter than the whole of the other. The "ball" might be an eighth note and the "change" a quarter note. Precede the Ball Change with a little kick of the "ball" foot for a "kick ball change."

Ballroom Dance Position – Standing and holding a partner in a traditional dance pose. Facing each other, the male places his right hand on the female's lower back and holds her right hand in his left. The female's left hand is placed on the back of his right shoulder. This position would be commonly used in such dances as the Waltz, Polka, Fox Trot, Tango, etc.

BALLROOM DANCE POSITION

Bow and Arrow Spin

Basic Soft Shoe – This very common sequence of steps used in the soft shoe is made up of a series of steps and ball changes. Facing front, the dancer steps left on the left foot followed by a ball change (right/left) with the ball being downstage left of the left foot. This occurs on beats 1 and 2. On beats 3 and 4, this same rhythmic step ball change is performed beginning with the right foot with the ball change consisting of a left/right combination toward downstage right. Beats 5-and-6-and-7-and-8 are made up of a step to the left with three ball changes: (1) right/left downstage left (2) right/left upstage right, (3) right/left downstage left. Usually this 8-beat pattern would then be mirrored beginning on the right foot downstage right.

BASIC SOFT SHOE

Beg Hands – Clasp your hands as though you are begging as if to ask "please?"

BEG HANDS

Blade Hands – A hand position in which all fingers are touching and the hand is as straight as possible. The palm can be facing any direction, which will usually be indicated in the directions. If it is not, it probably means that the palm is out toward the audience.

BLADE HANDS

Bow and Arrow Spin – Any variation of a spin around oneself. An example is to cross your right foot over your left on beats "and 1" then swivel around to the left in two or three more counts, tucking your elbows in close to your sides and using a combination of heel/toe weight changes with each foot to help you get around.

BOW AND ARROW SPIN

Box Step

Box Step
This is one of the more common patterns of walking steps used by song and dance artists. It consists of four steps. Step 1: The left foot steps directly downstage. Step 2: Bring the right foot across the left. Step 3: The left foot steps upstage of the crossed right. Step 4: Bring the right foot back to where it began to the right side of the left foot. This can be started on any one of the steps as long as the pattern is continued for at least four counts. It can easily be started on the right foot and reversed so that the left foot does the cross over on beat two.

With minor variations, the Box Step can be used in almost any style of dance. If the knees are turned out it begins to look country style. If a deep plié is used, it takes on a strong jazz feel. With knees picked up high on each step, it can add to a Charleston or Ragtime routine. The Box step is also often called a Jazz Square. The two terms are interchangeable, but Box Step is probably more common because it indicates a more versatile move.

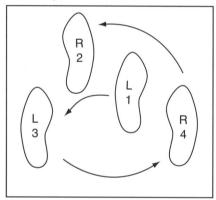
BOX STEP

Bravo Hands
Clasp hands, usually slightly above shoulder height, as in a gesture of "bravado."

BRAVO HANDS

Burst Clap
First the dancer reaches both jazz hands outstretched and overhead. (This may or may not be a full extension of the arms) Following this "burst" of outstretched hands, the dancer claps either overhead or at chest level.

BURST CLAP

Burst (High to Low/Low to High)
This is the action of bringing one's arms from overhead down to your sides. It can (but does not have to be) preceded by a clasping of the fists in preparation for bursting jazz hands that lower out to your sides. This can be done with a variety of hand positions from open jazz hands, palms up or palms down. Reverse the move to burst from low to high.

BURST (HIGH TO LOW/LOW TO HIGH)

Cabbage Patch — With straight arms and fists at about waist level simply stir those parallel arms in front of yourself in a circular motion once for every two counts. Your head and shoulders can turn in opposition to emphasize the move.

CABBAGE PATCH

California Raisins — All you do is:
Beat 1: Churn your traveling hands around each other like a referee calling a traveling violation in basketball. (Ask the kids.)
Beat 2: Simultaneously, snap the fingers of your left hand at your right elbow and the fingers of your right hand at about head level.
Beat 3: Repeat beat one with traveling hands.
Beat 4: Simultaneously, snap the fingers of your right hand at your left elbow and the fingers of your left hand at about head level.

CALIFORNIA RAISINS

Charleston — A lively ballroom dance of the 1920s in which the knees are twisted in and out and the heels are swung sharply outward on each step. The basic Charleston consists of one step touch to the front and one to the back with the palms of the hands showing to the audience and swinging from left to right and back.

CHARLESTON

Chassé — This is a French term for a dance step that consists of three steps in a dotted quarter note-eighth-quarter rhythm. The pattern is used to slide or glide across the floor.

Chugging Fists at Sides — With fists held at hip level and elbows bent at 90 degrees, accent those fists down toward the floor on each beat of the music.

CHUGGING FISTS AT SIDES

Chugs

Chugs – A dance step borrowed from the Charleston of the 1920s. The dancer jumps with both feet to one side and then to the other. You jump into the floor and bring your jazz hands from your thighs up to your chest level with each jump. This can also be performed in ballroom dance position with a partner.

CHUGS

Clap Burst – A clap followed by a burst of hands usually in a "jazz" position. Like fireworks, the jazz hands slowly drop to the sides after the energetic percussion of the clap.

CLAP BURST

Crocodile Smile – A dance step made popular in the *Hop 'Til You Drop* song collection. The dancers extend their arms fully out in front of them at about mouth level. Palms are together with one hand on top of the other. Then the dancer opens and shuts these straight arms like the jaws of a big crocodile.

CROCODILE SMILE

Disco Arms – With the L hand on the L hip, point the R finger up and to the right for two beats, then across the body and down to the left for two beats. Then up to the right for one beat, down to the left for one beat, up to the right for one beat, down to the left for one beat.

DISCO ARMS

Disco Hands – See **Pulp Fiction Hands**.

Do Si Do – Taken from country square dancing, the Do Si Do really means to just walk, skip or run around your partner. Usually this will be executed while circling each other. In other words, there will be a time when the partners are front to front, side to side, back to back, side to side and then front to front again in one complete Do Si Do revolution.

DO SI DO

Drag Step – While facing the audience, (1) take a big step with your left foot toward stage left. (2) Drag your right foot using a full two counts to do the drag. Then either step together or follow the drag step with a back step.

DRAG STEP

Drop Shoulders/Music Express Shoulders

– With feet apart and bent elbows at your side, accent your shoulders down four times as you lean to the left, turning slightly to face the right as you do so. Then do four shoulder drops as you lean to the right, facing slightly left as you do so.

DROP SHOULDERS/MUSIC EXPRESS SHOULDERS

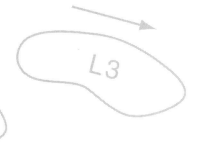

Feet Replacements – Put all of the weight onto your right foot and extend your left out to the side. The supporting leg is bent slightly. Shift your weight to the left foot as the right leg goes out to the side. Repeat this several times not letting your head go up and down as you "replace" one foot with the other.

FEET REPLACEMENTS

First Position – See Standing Positions (First/Second).

Flexed Foot – See Foot Positions (Flexed or Pointed).

Flick Kick – A two-count move that begins by stepping one direction as if you are going to run that way. Then you reverse direction and kick that same foot that you were stepping onto up and behind. That kicked foot will usually take on a "back attitude" position as it is kicked and you hop onto the other foot.

FLICK KICK

Foot Positions

Foot Positions (Flexed or Pointed) –
"Flexed" is the opposite of "pointed." The toes of the foot are brought up as close to the same shin as possible. "Pointed" foot is a more accurate way of instructing the dancers to use their entire foot to point as opposed to "pointing their toes." The whole foot works by extending the toes downward and the heel up. (Hint: To make the foot look even more pointed, bring the heel of that foot forward as you point the rest of it.)

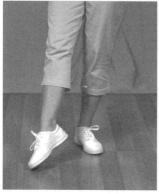

FOOT POSITIONS (POINTED)   **FOOT POSITIONS (FLEXED)**

Four Point Pivot – See Pivot (4-Point).

Funky Chicken – A ridiculous dance in which the performer flaps their elbows like the wings of a chicken and their knees like a cymbal playing a one-man band.

FUNKY CHICKEN

Gospel Style Step Touch – This step touch style is borrowed from the traditional Gospel style choir. It involves stepping one direction and then backing into that direction as you touch with the whole of the other foot. Then you repeat the move to the other side by backing into a step touch on the other side.

GOSPEL STYLE STEP TOUCH

Grapevine (8-count or 4-count) – An eight-count pattern of marching in which the shoulders of the dancer are square to the audience throughout. The first step is directly out to the side, followed by a step behind or in front, still moving in the same direction. Six more steps of similar nature alternating between steps behind and in front follow this. This can be used in almost all styles of music with the real character of the routine added from the waist up.

A shorter (4-count) version of the grapevine simply uses four counts of the longer version. In other words, (1) step out (2) cross in front or back (3) step out again (4) bring feet together.

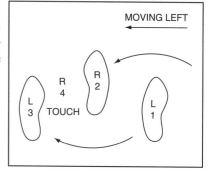

GRAPEVINE (4-COUNT)

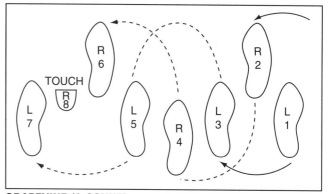

GRAPEVINE (8-COUNT)

Home Alone

Half Time March — Marching one step for every two beats. Usually, the feet are both on the ground for the actual step (beats 1 and 3) with alternating knees coming up on the off beats (2 and 4). The arms usually work with 90-degree elbows alternating to hold briefly at chest level on each step (1 and 3).

HALF TIME MARCH

Hand Jive — A 16-count clapping and slapping pattern made famous in the 1950s and '60s but well known even today.
1-2: Slap your thighs two times.
3-4: Clap twice
5-6: Slice your right hand two times over your left in a scissoring move.
7-8: Slice your left hand two times over your right in a scissoring move.
9-10: Pound your right fist on top of your left two times.
11-12: Pound your left fist on top of your right two times.
13-14: Accent your right thumb over your right shoulder two times.
15-16: Accent your left thumb over your left shoulder two times.

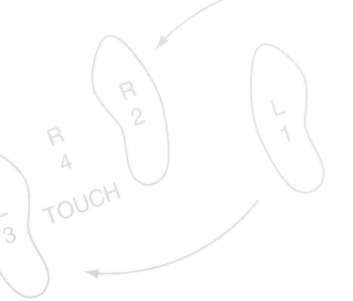

Heel Drags — A bit of a misnomer in that the "heel" is not being dragged so much as the whole of the opposite foot. It is a country or folk-type step that begins by stepping onto the heel of one foot with the toes in the air, then pulling the opposite foot along so that the feet come together. In other words, the pattern of this walking pattern is step (heel), "drag" in opposite foot. You will recognize this step as one often-used in country line dancing.

HEEL DRAGS

Hesitation Waltz — Like a regular waltz, this dance utilizes three whole counts. The difference is that on a regular waltz, the dancers steps three times, once for each quarter note. In a Hesitation Waltz, the dancers take the first two steps only and then hold still for the third. You can think of it as quarter note followed by a half. You might also see it in a Minuet.

HESITATION WALTZ

Home Alone — The dancer places both hands on the sides of their face and either silently or audibly opens their mouth like a loud "AH!" Use this funny gesture to show shock or surprise.

HOME ALONE

11

Jazz Hands

Jazz Hands – A hand position in which all of the fingers are spread generally as far as possible. The palm can be facing any direction. That will usually be indicated. If it is not, it probably means that the palm is out toward the audience.

JAZZ HANDS

Jerk – On beat 1, reach one hand over your head and the other somewhat behind your back while at the same time thrusting your chest and ribcage out in front of you to the side of the higher hand. On beat 2, throw both hands forward and violently bring the chest and ribcage to a contracted position.

JERK

Jitterbug – A traditional dance pattern that can be performed with or without a partner. It consists of a step (L), ball change (R L), step (R), ball change (L R), back step (L R). This would be counted "1 and 2, 3 and 4, 5 6." If you started the dance on beat 1 of four 4-beat measures, the accented L foot will be on a different beat of each ensuing measure until you have made an entire round. If this were performed in a traditional partnered ballroom dance formation, the female partner would begin the combination stepping onto the right foot.

JITTERBUG

Kick Ball Change – See **Ball Change/Kick Ball Change**.

Knee Pops Second Position – Standing in second position (feet apart), lift your heels off the floor so the knees pop out and apart. Note that your head and shoulders stay at the same level through out.

KNEE POPS SECOND POSITION

"L" Arms – A position of the arms in which they form the letter "L." One arm is toward the ceiling and one is parallel to the floor at shoulder level.

"L" ARMS

Lasso – Put one hand overhead and swing it around and around as if you were a cowboy swinging a rope.

LASSO

Lindy – A five-step move associated with swing music. A basic Lindy step consists of a Chassé followed by a back step. For instance, slide to the left in a dotted eighth-sixteenth-quarter pattern (L R L) and then a two quarter note back step (R L), keeping your shoulders square to the audience the entire time. Repeat the pattern to the other side. This can also be performed with a partner. Face each other and either hold hands or assume a ballroom dance position as you Lindy in the same direction.

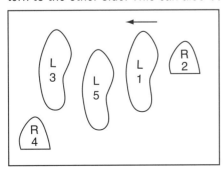
LINDY

Locomotion – Put a series of HEEL DRAGS and TRAIN ARMS together to do this dance from the 1960s.

LOCOMOTION

Major Whack Attack – See **Whack Attack (Major/Minor)**.

March – This simply instructs the dancer to walk to the beat of the music. It usually would suggest that the walk is a bit stronger than your usual stride, more like a soldier would walk to a cadence. It also suggests one step for each beat of the measure. A March tempo is generally assumed to be approximately quarter note = 120.

Mashed Potato – A silly dance of the 1950s and '60s in which the dancer keeps their knees together and elbows bent like the wings of a chicken. As the dancer flaps their elbows, they step down with one foot or the other as if they are "mashing potatoes" into the floor. Remember that the knees are together during this routine so it is only the lower part of the leg that is doing the bending and smashing. A common and interesting pattern for the Mashed Potato is to mash four times with the right foot, then four with the left, followed by two right, two left, then one a piece four times R, L, R, L.

MASHED POTATO

Minor Whack Attack – See **Whack Attack (Major/Minor)**.

Minuet – Facing your partner, place the female's right hand on top of the male's right hand. Utilizing a hesitation waltz pattern, step touch moving together and then apart like an old fashioned Minuet. This is a very formal dance. The women could hold their skirt with their free hand, and the men could place their free hand behind their back or hold the lapel of their jacket.

MINUET

Monkey – A comical dance from the 1960s in which the dancers imitate actual monkeys by swinging their straight arms up and down like a monkey climbing a tree. In variations, some dancers have been known to actually pretend to peel a banana or scratch their flea-ridden bodies.

MONKEY

Music Express Shoulders – See **Drop Shoulders**.

Opera Hands – Holding your hands clasped together at chest level in a caricature-like imitation of a formal opera singer or recitalist. One hand is on top of the other, clasped together with fingers to the inside of the opposite hand's knuckles.

OPERA HANDS

Paddle Wheel Turn – A series of step ball changes (usually four steps and three ball changes) that propel the dancer in a circle around oneself. It is almost as if one foot is nailed to the floor and the other is trying to go someplace. The result is that you move in circles. Recognized mostly in soft shoe style dances, the Paddlewheel turn can be adapted to almost any style or period from Country to Conga, Charleston to Jazz! The arms are often held straight in a diagonal pattern with the arm down the direction the dancer is turning.

PADDLE WHEEL TURN

Passé —The French term for a two-part move. (1) Lift the knee across the front and up toward the waist, and (2) point that same foot that was lifted out to its own side.

PASSÉ

Pas de bourrée — The French term for a three-step pattern that basically has one step going behind, the next almost in place, and the third back to second position. For instance, (1) step with the L foot as far to the right of the R foot as possible from behind, (2) step slightly forward with the R foot, and (3) step out to the left again with the L foot to resume your starting position, or lunge slightly to the left with that L foot.

Patty Cake — A partnered routine that resembles the child's game by the same name. One pattern is as follows (facing your partner):
1. Slap your legs.
2. Clap.
3. Hit right hands together.
4. Clap.
5. Hit left hands together.
6. Clap.
7. Hit both hands together.
8. Clap.

PATTY CAKE

Peel Off/Ripple — Any move that is done by each member of the cast in succession, like the "wave" a crowd does in a sports stadium. This move could be executed like the falling of a row of dominos by individuals or small groups perhaps on each beat of a measure, on the downbeat or in some other even sequence.

PEEL OFF/RIPPLE

Pivot (2-Point) — Four marching steps that allow the dancers to do a complete turn around and end up at the same place they started. (1) Step straight ahead with the L foot, (2) pivot 180 degrees to the right and step toward the back wall with R foot, (3) step toward the back wall with the L foot, (4) pivot 180 degrees to the right and step toward the front with the R foot, so that you are back to where you began.

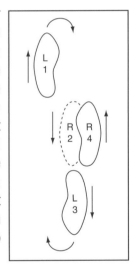
PIVOT (2-POINT)

Pivot (4-Point)

Pivot (4-Point) – An eight-step move that involves two steps toward each wall with the performer making one complete turn around but not actually going any place. Each quarter turn happens as a pivot on one foot, for example the left, if you are actually turning to your left.

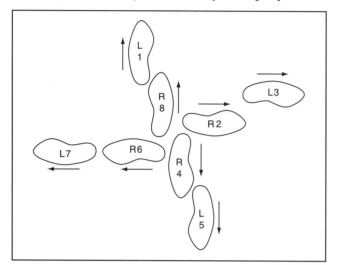

PIVOT (4-POINT)

Plié – The French term for bending your knees. It is considered the opposite of relevé.

PLIÉ

Pointed Foot – See Foot Positions (Flexed or Pointed).

Polka – A dance familiar to European and Scandinavian folk dances, three steps and a hop make up a basic Polka step. It can be performed individually, in a traditional ballroom dance position with a partner, with elbows linked or with many other variations. This is generally considered a lively dance full of spins, covering considerable territory.

Pony – Basically a Polka for the 1950s through the 1970s, this is also a three-step pattern in which the dancer hops onto one foot and quickly follows with a ball and change. There are many variations for the hands including holding the reins of an imaginary pony, pretending to swing a lasso, or even pretending to use a riding crop on your imaginary horse.

PONY

Prayer Hands – Hold your straight hands together with fingers pointed toward the ceiling as if you are in a position of prayer.

PRAYER HANDS

Present Arms (High/To Audience/Low)

– This definition is borrowed from game show models whose job it is to "present" the prizes behind revealing doors or curtains. They usually move their upturned palms with a straight arm across the space of the prize. So if the direction is to "present the audience," the dancer may move their right hand from stage L to R at about chest level. "Present arms" could also be a more stationary position. If the directions are to "present high," the dancer simply raises their straight arms overhead in a "Y" pattern. Usually, there will be a more specific direction as to the exact position of the hands. For instance, "present jazz hands low" would tell the dancer to extend both arms out to the sides, front and lower than the waist with spread fingers, palms out toward the audience. There are almost unlimited variations of Present Arms.

PRESENT ARMS (HIGH/TO AUDIENCE/LOW)

Pulp Fiction Hands (Disco Hands) –

Bend the knees and while keeping your left hand on the left knee, move the right hand with "V" finger, palm out, across the eyes from left to right. Then switch to the other side.

PULP FICTION HANDS (DISCO HANDS)

Push Steps (Squish a Bug)

– A funky two-count move that resembles the squishing of a bug out to the dancer's side. Facing the audience, on beat 1 the dancer pushes the foot directly out to the side utilizing the ball and toes of the foot only. As the dancer does this, their shoulder will turn away from that pushed foot. If the left foot is pushed out to the left, the shoulder will turn so that the upper body faces somewhat stage right. Only partial weight is put on that stepping foot with most of the weight remaining on the stationary left. The second move brings that pushed foot back to its starting position (feet together) and shoulder again square to the audience. Try it to the other side and alternate it back and forth for a fun and funky dance routine.

PUSH STEPS (SQUISH A BUG)

Rainbow Arms

– Using a straight arm with the palm down, make one complete rotation of that arm across the front of your body. The arm begins in a downward motion across the front, moves out to the opposite side, overhead and to the same side as the "moving" arm and back down to the side where it began. It is simply a 180-degree or a 360-degree circle of the arm with the performer facing the audience the entire time. The "rainbow" analogy comes from the overhead arch that the arm and hand makes as it completes the top half of the rotation. It is an effective move when the dancer wants to accentuate lyrics about the sky, the world, space, everything or everywhere, etc.

RAINBOW ARMS

Rah! Rah! Fist – Swing your fist across the front of your body at about waist level with the elbow bent at 90 degrees like a cheerleader as they accent their cheer.

RAH! RAH! FIST

Relevé – This is a French term that essentially means pushing up from your heels so that you are standing on the balls of your feet or even your tip toes. This is the opposite of Plié.

RELEVÉ

Rubber Legs – Stand with your feet shoulder width apart and slightly bent knees with the weight on the balls of your feet. Flap your legs together and apart as if they were rubbery.

RUBBER LEGS

"S" Pose – In various degrees, this is a stance in which the dancer's feet are together with one foot and leg slightly in front (downstage) of the other. The shoulders remain square to the audience and there is a natural "S" line that runs up the forward leg, across the hip, waist, chest and shoulder. The hands are held either on the hip, overhead, down at the sides or in some other variation. This is the traditional pose of showgirls, models or even body builders because it is a flattering stance on almost all types of bodies.

"S" POSE

Salute (3-Count) – A stagy salute in which beat 1 has the dancer bringing their right hand to their forehead while at the same time bending both knees slightly. On beat 2, the legs straighten up and the right hand goes straight up overhead with fingers still tightly together and outstretched. On beat 3, the arm and hand come back to their side.

SALUTE (3-COUNT)

Scissors Hands – Like the movement of a large scissors, the dancer moves their hands and arms back and forth, one over the other. In this case the accent is usually put where the hands are crossed as opposed to when they are open.

SCISSORS HANDS

Scoop Hands – With palms up, bring your straight arms from low by the sides of your leg to overhead. It's as if you are scooping up something or lifting something to overhead.

SCOOP HANDS

Second Position – See **Standing Positions (First/Second)**.

Skate – The dancers pretend to be ice-skating or roller-skating. To accentuate the move, as you step onto one foot lift the other behind in a 90 degree attitude. Hands can be held behind the back, inside a real or imaginary muff, or held in the hands of a partner.

SKATE

Sleep Hands – With hands held together like you are going to pray (extended fingers), place both hands under your cheek of your face and tilt your head slightly to that side as if your hands were a pillow.

SLEEP HANDS

Snake

Snake – A 1980s move in which the dancer ripples their entire body toward one side of the stage or the other beginning with the top of their head and isolating each part of the body so that it sequences all the way down to the feet. Usually it is performed with shoulders basically square to the audience. For instance, leaning toward the left, lunge with top of the head followed by L shoulder, L side of rib cage, L waist, L hips, and L leg. Repeat to the right.

SNAKE

Snow Hands – Start with jazz hands extended overhead and lower them while wiggling your fingers. You are indicating snow falling.

SNOW HANDS

Smurf – This consists of a four-count grapevine step that ends with a hitching up of the knee as opposed to a touch. For example, if you are beginning the step moving to the left with your shoulders square to the audience, you would step first onto your left foot, cross behind or in front with the right on 2, again to the left on 3 and then hitch up your right knee to about waist high on 4. Repeat to the other side.

BEAT 4 OF THE SMURF

Spinners/Temptations Pushes – A routine in which the dancers hold both fists at 90-degree angles at their sides. Then they step left and bring their feet together as they push those fists in that direction. A common pattern would include two pushes left, two pushes right and then one a piece, four more times.

SPINNERS/TEMPTATIONS PUSHES

Spirit of '76 March – A march pattern in which the dancer uses one stiff leg with a very flat foot and the other stepping only on the ball of the foot, so there is a natural up/down look to the march. It is supposed to resemble a soldier who is wounded and has one leg in a cast, unable to bend it. The "Spirit of '76" is a famous painting of three Revolutionary war soldiers marching along with a flag, a fife and a drum. This march helps to capture that spirit.

SPIRIT OF '76 MARCH

Stand By Position – Feet together, hands held in the small of your back so that there is space between your elbows and your sides, chin up, big smile.

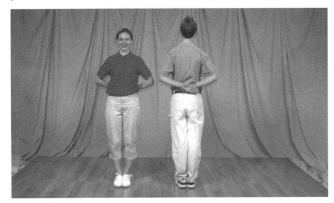

STAND BY POSITION

Squish a Bug – See Push Steps.

Standing Positions (First/Second) – First position means standing with your feet together, heels touching, and toes apart. A "parallel first" would mean that the heels and toes are together.

Second position means feet apart. On occasion there may be more specific directions such as "parallel second" which would indicate that the feet should be pointed straight ahead and no further apart than the heels. A "turned out second" would mean that the feet are apart with the toes actually further apart than the heels.

Starburst – A group of dancers standing in a clump or in rows each presents their jazz hands to the audience with arms outstretched from the center of the group. The front rows obviously must be low, the back rows high and the side rows out to their respective sides. The result is a group pose that appears to have rays of light emanating from the center of the group.

STARBURST

Step Clap – Step to one side followed by a clap usually to that same side. For instance, step left on beat 1 and clap either on the offbeat or on beat 2 also to the left. Repeat to the other side.

Step Dig – See Step Touch.

Step Kick

Step Kick (SL KR, etc. or L KR R KL, etc.) –
Step on one foot followed by a kick of the other foot. The abbreviations indicate which foot you are stepping onto and which one you are kicking. S = step, K = kick, L = left, R = right.

STEP KICK

Step Stomp – See Step Touch.

Step Scuff – Step on one foot and follow that with a scuff of the opposite heel off the floor in front of the "stepping" foot. It's as if you are saying, "Awe shucks!" Repeat to the other side. This works for soft shoe or easy swing-type dance routines.

STEP SCUFF

Step Touch/Step Dig/Step Stomp – Step with one foot followed by a touch of the other foot on the ground next to the first step. Another way to describe this is sometimes "step-together." The touch can be varied with a "dig" with the foot in back of the step foot, or a stomp with the foot in front of the step foot.

STEP DIG

STEP STOMP

Stop March – As if you were going to begin marching, lift your left knee up and bring it down so that it reaches the floor on beat 1. Freeze at that moment of contact, so that you basically just stomp the foot on the floor next to the other foot. The arms will move similarly in that they wind up as if to begin a march and then down to a stiff standstill at your sides on the stomp.

Stroll – An eight-count grapevine step, or series of steps that was a popular group dance in the 1950s and 1960s. In this dance the grapevine is often executed while facing a partner and moving through two parallel lines of dancers that are forming a lane in the middle of the dance floor.

Sugar Foot – Standing with your feet apart and on the balls of both feet, twist back and forth with each step that you take. The toes of both feet are facing in the same direction on each step as if you are squashing something under your feet. This is a 1940s move appropriate to the Jitterbug and Lindy.

SUGAR FOOT

Sway (Leading with Shoulder) – Rock your entire body from side to side either from a standing, sitting or kneeling position. Usually the sway is performed by leading with the shoulder in the direction you are moving.

SWAY (LEADING WITH SHOULDER)

Sway Snap– A step touch in which both hands swing the direction you are stepping and then snap on that side as you touch together. Everything is moving in the same direction.

SWAY SNAP

Swing Your Partner – Taken from square dancing routines, face your partner and link same elbows (e.g. R) so that your R shoulders are together. Run, walk or skip around each other, held together by your own elbows. Reverse and link L elbows and circle the opposite direction.

SWING YOUR PARTNER

Swivel Both Knees

Swivel Both Knees – With your feet and legs held tightly together, bend your knees and make one complete revolution as they both move in the same direction. Try moving them down to the right, down center, down to the left and back to standing up straight in one fluid motion.

SWIVEL BOTH KNEES

Temptations Pushes –
See **Spinners/Temptations Pushes**.

Three-Count Salute – See Salute (3-Count).

Three-Point Turn – See Turn (3-Point).

Tilting Hand Claps – Simply clap on every beat and as you do so your hands tilt in front of your body the direction of your clap.

TILTING HAND CLAPS

Train Arms – With 90 degree bent elbows; churn them by your sides like the wheels of an old-fashioned railroad train. Use in combination with Train Step.

TRAIN ARMS

Train Step – (1) Step forward with your left foot, (2) back with your right, (3) further back with your left, and (4) forward with your right. In actuality, the right foot is stepping in the same place both times but because of the forward and backward nature of the left foot, it seems that the right is moving back and forth, too. The feet movement looks like a train wheel cranking along. Use in combination with Train Arms.

TRAIN STEP

Travel or Traveling Arms – Churning your fists around each other in a rapid fashion, just like a basketball referee does when he calls a "traveling violation," two counts left and then two counts right in a 4/4 measure. This hand move has a distinctive Latin feel, but can also work in Rock and Roll, and other places.

TRAVEL OR TRAVELING ARMS

Triplet Pats – Pat your thighs with your open hand in a triplet pattern (one and a).

TRIPLET PATS

Truckin' – With the index finger of one hand held in the air, the dancer step-hops either in place or moving. The dancer leads slightly with their chest in the direction of the step-hop, and then repeats to the other side. This step is used often in dances of the 1930s–1950s.

TRUCKIN'

Turn (3-Point) – This turn involves one complete revolution that takes 3 steps to accomplish while the dancer continues to move in the direction they are turning. For example, as they use three steps to turn to their left, they are also moving further toward stage left. There is no turn on step 1 (L foot out to side L). On 2 (R foot and body cross in front) the dancer should be halfway around and facing upstage. On 3 (L foot and body continues around) the dancer is again facing front.

Two Point Pivot – See **Pivot (2-Point)**.

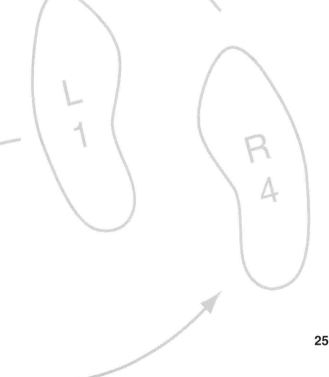

U Dip

U Dip – With your feet apart, plié deeply (bend your knees) and then straighten them up so that you are putting your weight on the left foot and are facing stage right. Repeat to the other side by again bending your knees and then straightening them so that the weight goes to the right foot and you face stage left. The motion of bending and straightening causes the dancer to make a "U" with their entire body, thus the name of the step. Notice the feet never lose contact with the ground and are in the same place throughout the U Dip. There are no "steps" involved, only weight changes and body angles.

U DIP

U Steps – Keeping your body square to the audience, perform a step touch pattern (step together). As you step, bend your knees and as you bring your feet together, straighten your legs so that the body has made a "U" in the air. Notice that the difference between this step and a U Dip is that on a U Step the dancer is actually moving their feet. It truly is a U Step. Also there is no turning of the body angle.

U STEPS (DOWN)   **U STEPS (UP)**

Vaudeville Rocks – With jazz hands held at about shoulder level and facing toward the audience, the dancer rocks the entire body, especially the hands and hips, left and right with a lot of energy. A variation would be to raise the jazz hands so they were actually waving overhead as the body rocks left and right.

VAUDEVILLE ROCKS

Walk In a Circle Around Yourself – In as many counts as the music allows (usually 4, 6, or 8), walk in a circle around an imaginary pole and end up right back where you started.

Walking Knee Pops – With your feet together, alternate bending one knee and then the other so they pop out in front of you. It is as if you were walking without even picking up your feet. This can look either funky, Latin, smooth or many other ways depending on the tempo and style in which you walk.

WALKING KNEE POPS

Whack Attack (Major/Minor*)
—This is a fun name for any series of claps and slaps that constitute a body percussion routine. Usually a Major Whack Attack includes at least eight counts to the pattern. One simple "whack attack routine" would be:
1. Clap.
2. Slap your R leg with your R hand.
3. Slap your L leg with your L hand.
4. Clap.
5. Hit your L heel with your R hand.
6. Slap your L leg with your L hand.
7. Slap your R leg with your R hand.
8. Clap.
9. Slap your L cheek with your L hand. (Not too hard!)
10. Slap your R check with your R hand. (Not too hard!)
11. Slap your L leg with your L hand.
12. Slap your R leg with your R hand.
13-16. Clap four times with each clap getting higher.

*A Minor Whack Attack could simply be the first four counts of this pattern.

Windmill Arms — See Wraps/Windmill arms.

Winnie The Pooh Hips
— With feet apart and knees slightly bent, swing your hips from side to side. Hold your fists on your hips as you do so.

WINNE THE POOH HIPS

Wipe
— Slice your hands once like an umpire does when he calls a runner "safe" in baseball. A natural move that indicates "No way!"

WIPE

Wraps
— With both arms moving simultaneously from one side to the other, they begin by being wrapped around your waist, the right arm in front and the left behind. They then reach high above your head in as big an arch as possible until they get to the other side and end up with the left arm wrapped across the front of the waist and the right arm behind.

WRAPS

Windmill Arms
— Similar to the wrap, Windmill Arms are slower and are often used in a peel off or ripple. Start with arms wrapped around waist, the right in front and the left behind. Then reach up high with the right hand followed by the left hand in a big arch over the head. End with the left arm wrapped across the front of the waist and the right arm behind.

WINDMILL ARMS

CHARADES

Directions:
1) Make a copy of these words and phrases and cut them up into strips of paper.
2) Put the pieces of paper into a hat or bowl.
3) Divide the classroom into two teams.
4) Take turns having one member of each team step to the front of the room, draw a slip of paper out of the hat and perform the word or phrase that they have chosen. The team they represent must try to guess what the move or combination is. You can time them and see who can get the answers the fastest.

Do the Axle	**Choose a partner and present a Ballroom Dance Position**
Do a Back Step (BS)	**Perform the Basic Soft Shoe**
Do a Kick Ball Change (KBC)	**Show Begging Hands**

Show Prayer Hands	Burst (High to Low then Low to High)
Demonstrate Bravo Hands	Do the Cabbage Patch
Demonstrate Sleep Hands	Do four California Raisins
Do a Box Step	Do the Charleston
Do a Burst Clap	Do a Chassé

Step touch with chugging fists at your sides	**Do a Drag Step**
Do some Chugs	**Perform a 4-count Grapevine**
Do a Clap Burst	**Perform an 8-count Grapevine**
Do the Crocodile Smile	**Do some Feet Replacements**
Choose a partner and Do Si Do	**Show a Flexed Foot**

Show a Pointed Foot	Do the Hand Jive
Execute a Flick Kick	Do some Heel Drags
Do the Funky Chicken	Choose a partner and do the Hesitation Waltz
Demonstrate the Gospel Style Step Touch	Home Alone
Do a Half Time March	Show your Jazz Hands

Do the Jerk	**Do the Locomotion**
Do the solo Jitterbug Step	**March**
Do some Knee Pops in second position	**Do the Mashed Potato**
Show your "L" arms	**Choose a partner and do the Minuet**
Do the Lindy	**Do the Monkey**

Drop Shoulders **(Music Express Shoulders)**	**Choose a partner and** **do the Patty Cake**
Bow and Arrow Spin	**Show a Pas de bourré**
Show Opera Hands	**Make the class do a Peel Off**
Do a Paddle Wheel Turn	**Make the class do a Ripple**
Show a Passé	**Do a 2-Point Pivot**

Do a 4-Point Pivot	**Demonstrate Second Position**
Demonstrate a Plié	**Present Arms high**
Choose a partner and do the Polka	**Present Arms low**
Do the Pony	**Push Steps (Squish a Bug)**
Demonstrate First Position	**Do Rainbow Arms**

Rah! Rah! Fist	**Scoop Hands**
Do a Relevé	**Show Snow Hands**
Show your Rubber Legs	**Do the Skate**
Do an "S" pose	**Do Spinners/Temptations Pushes**
Do a Salute (3 count)	**Show the Spirit of '76 March**

Demonstrate Stand By Position	**Step Touch**
Choose at least two partners and do Starburst	**Step Dig**
Step Clap	**Step Stomp**
Step Kick	**Stop March**
Step Scuff	**Do the Sugar Foot**

Sway **(leading with shoulder)**	**Swivel both knees**
Sway Snap	**Do the Smurf**
Swing Your Partner	**Do the Stroll**
Lasso	**Train Step with Train Arms**
Do the Snake	**Travel Arms**

Three Point Turn	U Dip
Tilting Hand Claps	U Step
Triplet Pats	Do some Vaudeville Rocks
Truckin'	Walk in a Circle Around Yourself
Two Point Pivot	Do some Walking Knee Pops

Do a Major Whack Attack	**Wipe with Scissors Hands**
Do a Minor Whack Attack	**Do some Wraps or Windmill Arms**
Show Your Winnie the Pooh Hips	*More advanced combinations* **Lindy L, Lindy R, end with 3-count Salute**
More advanced combinations **3-point turn L, then R, end with Begging Hands**	*More advanced combinations* **Drag step L, 3-point turn R**
More advanced combinations **Do four Marches followed by a 2-point Pivot**	*More advanced combinations* **Lindy L, 3-point turn R**

More advanced combinations

**Do Traveling Arms
L, R, L, R, low to high
and Present High**

More advanced combinations

**Do four Step Claps,
3-point turn L, Drag Step R**

More advanced combinations

**Do four Step Kicks and
one 2-point Pivot**

More advanced combinations

**Hop on one foot while
doing the Crocodile Smile**

More advanced combinations

**Walk in a circle around
yourself L, then do a
Major Whack Attack**

**Make Up Your
Own Combination!**

**Make Up Your
Own Combination!**

**Make Up Your
Own Combination!**

**Make Up Your
Own Combination!**

**Make Up Your
Own Combination!**